IMAGES
of England

SITTINGBOURNE

The Co-op butchers in East Street standing next to the Wheatsheaf public house. In the 1950s the top floor was used as a function hall for weddings and parties. The building is now occupied by the Action Plumbing Centre.

IMAGES
of England

SITTINGBOURNE

Compiled by
Ken and Ann Fosbraey

TEMPUS

First published 1995
Reprinted 1999
Copyright © Ken and Ann Fosbraey, 1995

Tempus Publishing Limited
The Mill, Brimscombe Port,
Stroud, Gloucestershire, GL5 2QG

ISBN 0 7524 0303 6

Typesetting and origination by
Tempus Publishing Limited
Printed in Great Britain by
Midway Clark Printing, Wiltshire

Contents

Acknowledgements

We would very much like to thank the Staff of Sittingbourne Library for their kind help and encouragement especially Sue Samson, Hazel Stanley, Carole Millen and Margaret Brice, before she moved to Gillingham Library. Our thanks also go to John Crunden, Morris Snashall and Sean Caveney who are members of the Swale Postcard Club, which is held in Sittingbourne, for the loan of some of their postcards.

We would also like to thank Alan Amos, Peter Morgan, the Staff of the *Sittingbourne East Kent Gazette* and any one else who has given any help or encouragement to us.

Another thank you goes to past photographers and authors for the wealth of history they left for future generations.

Time somehow seems to fly at Sittingbourne. — come and test it.

Introduction

To suggest that Sittingbourne is essentially a place to pass through reveals much about its historical significance. The town does in fact owe its very existence to those whose business led them to travel between London and the Continent of Europe in years gone by. When Milton, its neighbour to the north, enjoyed fame as a royal manor and substantial fishing port, Sittingbourne was little more than a small village situated alongside the main road. As such, it could easily have been dismissed and forgotten, but the story was only beginning.

This book of postcards and photographs is not the product of years of dull research, but of Ken and Ann's enthusiasm for the town and its people. In choosing not just to "pass through", but to spend their lives in Sittingbourne, they have discovered something of the richness of its social history which they hope to share in the following pages.

It was the Romans who must first have become familiar with the area as they constructed the original military road linking London with the key coastal ports of Dover and Richborough. Form this time on, travellers would have stopped to refresh themselves at Sittingbourne's two streams which flowed across the road, to the east of the junction of Bell Road with East Street, and to the west at the junction of St Michael's Road with West Street. Small settlements grew around these fords, but there was little growth until medieval times when pilgrims began to flock to Canterbury to visit the shrine of the murdered Thomas Becket. Sittingbourne's inhabitants seized this opportunity to make a living and roadside inns opened up to meet the constant demand for rest and refreshment.

As the number of pilgrims decreased, the town played host not only to discontented rebels and soldiers in more troubled times, but to Kings and Queens, including Henry VIII, in more prosperous years. During the sixteenth century, Sittingbourne became renowned for its coaching inns and served as an important staging post where horses were changed over.

With the coming of the railway, the town's character was transformed. Now travellers could pass through without the need to stope, but others were attracted to the town to find work. Bricks and cement, the famous Thames spit-sail barges and paper-making developed into important industries and Sittingbourne became home for many ordinary men and women, whose way of life is illustrated in this publication.

The authors have spent the past fifteen years collecting postcards and items of interest relating to Sittingbourne and the local area, and become increasingly fascinated by their discoveries. As you browse through the pages, they invite you to share their enthusiasm and to explore something of the living history of the town and work, wartime and peacetime, and of the countryside around must surely encourage us to enquire, to investigate and to begin our own journeys of discovery.

Sue Samson

One
The Main Road from Snips Hill to Keycol Hill

From the top of Snips Hill looking towards the town centre. On the left is a line of trees which disappeared long ago and standing next to them is Mr Holdstock's Garage which has been replaced by Echo House. On the right, where the Council's road sweeper cart is standing, is the opening to Harold Road.

Going towards Snips Hill in 1915 with Mr Holdstock's Garage on the right. There are a lot of children in this picture – perhaps they are on their way to school? At the top of the hill on the left is the Prince of Wales public house.

East Street with Mr Wade's butchers shop on the right, which is now owned by the Tudor Bathroom Centre. The building beyond that is No 149 which was Mr Newby's greengrocers shop but has now been demolished to make way for the roundabout.

This is a Sale of Work in the 1940s, possibly consisting of handy craft products which had been made by the ladies and some jumble sale items. It was held at the Methodist church in East Street opposite the Wheatsheaf public house.

The Co-op cake shop in East Street. It must have been near Easter as they are advertising for people to order their hot cross buns early. The shop now belongs to E Coomes Ltd, the bookmakers.

Sittingbourne Co-operative Society shops at 121-27 East Street stood next to the Methodist church. This building and the one on the next page were both demolished at the end of 1994, there is now only an empty space waiting to be built on.

This is the opening day of the Co-op's new shop in East Street on Saturday 5 May 1928. It was built of local bricks, had a white marble frontage and cost around £12,000 to build. Across the top of the centre arcade was the word PERSEVERANCE which may have been their motto.

The first cinema in Sittingbourne was the Empire in East Street, opened in 1910. In 1937 the name was changed to the Plaza but it was demolished in 1975 and Plaza Court now stands on the site.

WE'RE GOING TO BE RICH

This is the fervent hope

of all of us; so why not

join your friends at the

**PLAZA,
SITTINGBOURNE**

On Monday, November 28th,

or any day that week and

see

Gracie Fields and Victor McLaglen

in

"WE'RE GOING TO BE RICH"

A card advertising a film to be shown at the Plaza. On its other side is a photo of Gracie Fields.

East Street looking towards Snips Hill in the 1920s. On the left you can just see the old Drill Hall which is now the Pentecostal Church and on the right is the entrance to the Chestnut's doctors surgery.

Looking west along East Street. On the right is Thomasson the newsagents shop and on the left is the Old Oak public house.

At the crossroads in the High Street where Bell Road meets Crown Quay Lane. There were no traffic lights then so there is a policemen on point duty, wearing his white arm bands to direct the traffic. Standing on the right is the building which preceded the Odeon Cinema.

The Odeon Cinema opened on 4 January 1937 and the first film to be shown was *Little Lord Fauntleroy*. The cinema has now become the Cannon.

St Michael's church is the oldest church in Sittingbourne, dated from the thirteenth century. In 1762 workmen repairing the lead on the roof caused a bad fire. Restoration work was started the following year and the church was re-opened five years after the fire.

This beautiful snow scene postcard dated 26 December 1906 would make a lovely Christmas card.

The High Street in 1928. On the right is John Whibley General Drapers, Hosiery, Hatters and Outfitters shop which was noted for its household linen. The shop is now occupied by Iceland Frozen Foods.

Looking east down the High Street. On the left of the pavement is a lamp post with a notice board on it pointing to the Swimming Baths through Does Alley.

The Wesleyan church was opened in 1863 and it was almost destroyed in 1944 when it was bombed during the War. In the eighteenth century the house of William Doe stood on the forecourt of the church and when it was demolished the alley running along the side of the church was named Does Alley. On 11 October 1952 the new Wesleyan church was opened in place of the old one.

Facing west along the High Street in 1914. One the left is the George Hotel which had stabling and a coach house and later provided good accommodation for cyclists.

Parked on the left is a lovely old motorbike and sidecar – the year is 1922. Up the steps was the Registry Office which is now Harris and Harris, the Solicitors.

The Bull Hotel was licensed by the monks of Chilham Castle in the twelfth century and in 1954 it was modernised to combine the old with the new and it also became a free house.

The High Street facing east in 1926. On the left is the Rose Inn which is now the Wimpy Bar. Next door is the building one known as Rose Place. These premises once belonged to Millens Drapery Department, R Robinson, a chemist and Gorleys grocery shop – now some of it belongs to Woolworths.

A view of the High Street in 1916. On the left is Martins bank and the Lion Yard opening onto the Lion Hotel. Across the road a hardware shop with all the wares hanging outside.

Brenchley House, No 75 High Street in 1910. It was once used as a girls school. A little further along stands the lovely old building of the Town Hall.

The Town Hall standing proudly in the town centre in the 1930s. It was first used as a corn exchange but in 1878 was bought for use as the Town Hall. Sadly it was demolished in 1969 and the Westminster Bank now stands on the site. Further along is the Congregational church, long before Central Avenue was constructed.

On the right of this 1923 view can be seen Hogwoods Tea Rooms. There is an advertisement on the window for Frys Chocolate and three shops further down is a hairdressers and wig makers.

The Congregational church in the High Street at the turn of the century. The second shop on the left of the church is now the Leeds and on the other side of the alley is a butchers shop. It is interesting to note the big old steps that lead from the road to the pavement.

On the left of this 1915 view is the Maypole grocery shop, after than came a chemist shop and down a bit was No 78 which was May & Sayers outfitters shop.

The High Street facing west. On the right is David Greig's grocery shop where cake was cut to size from the slab and biscuits were taken from the tins, weighed and put in a paper bag.

Looking east from the Post Office in 1922 (the same motorbike and sidecar also appeared on page 20). It is our belief that it belonged to the photographer – the number on the motorbike is F.5095.

The Post Office standing on the left opened in 1911, closed in January 1961 and was demolished the same year. Now standing on the site is Halfords and Argos.

The Baptist tabernacle and memorial hall in the west end of the High Street in 1907. General Booth payed a visit here in 1905.

Looking east along the High Street about the 1920s. The house on the right is where the Pizzaland shop now stands and on the left is the well-known shop of Mr Dolding the Outfitters.

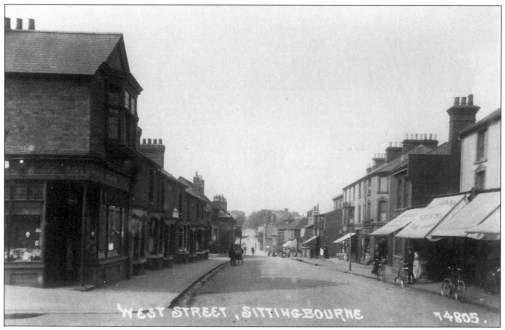

West Street in 1912. On the left is the entrance to Park Road and on the right, between the gap in the shops, just past the lamp post, is the opening of Dover Street.

Looking west towards Hollybank Hill. The Convent School is on the left and the building jutting out on the right is the Ebenezer Gospel Hall that which built in 1903. At one time it was used by the Salvation Army but it was pulled down around 1972.

The Roman Catholic church began in 1892 with a house for the priest and a schoolroom which was also used for church services. The church was opened in 1902.

The Sacred Heart Roman Catholic church in West Street began in 1892 and recently celebrated its Centenary. This postcard is dated 16 July 1906.

Hollybank Hill, looking east in 1919. Little has changed except for an increase in traffic and the house at the bottom of the hill on the left has been replaced by a garage.

Looking up Hollybank Hill towards West Street in 1916. How strange it looks with just the one house standing on the right which was used by the Armed Forces during the First World War.

London Road facing down Hollybank to the Kingshead public house on the right. On the opposite side of the road, past the telegraph pole, there is another public house called the King William IV which disappeared many years ago.

A GLIMPSE OF THE GARDENS

CONISTON HOTEL, SITTINGBOURNE

(OPEN TO NON-RESIDENTS)   KENT   Telephone : SITTINGBOURNE 7

How the Coniston Hotel in the London Road used to look in its early days before its extension, driveway and car park.

Rhode House once stood in the London Road at the corner of Staplehurst Road but it was demolished to make way for the Rhode House service station.

The British Queen in Key Street in the early 1900s stands opposite the Grove. Its name has now been changed to the Long Hop.

The Methodist chapel in Key Street held its last service on Sunday 27 March 1966 and was later demolished.

Key Street in 1922 showing the end part of the Grove on the left. Once again the old motorbike and sidecar have got into the picture.

Key Street in the early days when the Key public house was still standing on the corner of the road that leads to Sheerness. There was no need for traffic lights or roundabouts at the cross roads then.

Key Street facing towards Keycol Hill after the traffic lights were installed but before the roundabout was constructed. The garage standing on the left has now been demolished.

Key Street roundabout with its flower beds in 1993 – built to replace the traffic lights.

Keyhol Hill Hospital was built around 1880 as an isolation hospital for infectious diseases, many years later a sanatorium was added and in 1928 a new electrical plant was installed.

The women's chalet at the hospital for convalescence.

Two
The Streets and Roads of Sittingbourne

The opening of the Co-op at Nos 4-6 Station Street in 1904. It is nice to see the clothes they wore in those days and their fine show of hats. The shop is no longer there as it was demolished along with the rest of that side of Station Street in 1973.

St Michael's Vicarage was a gift from the Archbishop of Canterbury together with 1 1/2 acres of Glebe land. It was demolished in 1959 to make way for part of St Michael's Road and the houses that were originally built for the firemen.

Round the other side of the vicarage. How nice it looked with its walls covered in climbing plants and its lovely neat flower garden.

The bottom of Park Road as it joins the High Street in 1910. Standing on the immediate left is the old police station.

Looking up Park Road in 1922. It must have been nice and peaceful in those days without all the traffic that uses the road today.

About halfway up Park Road stands the Park Tavern public house. Judging by the caption on the postcard it came within the boundary of Milton.

Coming down Park Road towards the High Street in 1920. On the right there is a coalman with his horse and cart on his delivery round.

Standing in Bell Road at the corner of Highsted Road is the Memorial Hospital which was opened on 20 September 1930 by Mrs Garwood in memory of her parents Mr and Mrs Frank Lloyd.

Remembrance Avenue, Sittingbourne

The trees on each side of Remembrance Avenue were planted in 1923 in memory of the men of the town who sacrificed their lives for their country during the First World War.

College Road. Although in Sittingbourne, it came under the boundary of Milton Regis and is on the Barrow Grove Estate. This photograph shows the newly-built houses around 1930.

Written on this postcard is "they call it Tunstall Avenue but it is now Park Avenue as it is part of Gore Court Park". The old Gore Court Hall stood at the end of the avenue and this was the drive that led to the hall which has been pulled down.

Standing in Dover Street is the Holy Trinity church which was built of Kentish ragstone. Many of its windows were blown out in 1940 but services continued to be held.

This is how the inside of the church looked in 1915 with its lovely stone arches on each side of the centre aisle.

Dover Street in 1907. On the far left is the Fleur-De-Liz public house which was demolished around 1971. A veterinary surgery now stands in its place and there is a one-way system running through the street.

Victoria Road in 1908. This road runs along the side of the Coniston Hotel and leads into Wellwinch Road.

Three
Milton

In the centre of this greetings postcard is the Wyvern which is the crest of Milton Regis. On the left is Milton Holy Trinity church and on the right is Milton High Street which looks quite busy even though it was before the days of motor traffic. Underneath is a lovely sight of the Creek when it was still in constant use for transporting bricks, cement, paper and many other things.

Milton High Street showing the old Town Hall which was built in 1803. The public library now stands on its site. On the near-side of the Town Hall is Mr Shilling's shop.

In the right hand corner of this picture is Milton Post Office which has since been moved to the other side of the road.

Milton High Street in 1913. The big house on the left at the end of the street once belonged to the Hinde family and was known as Hinde House before it became Burleys Flats.

In 1937 Milton Post Office was a shop belonging to Madame Young.

School children of Milton are all gathered in Milton High Street to see the Duke of York's visit to the area on 14 July 1921.

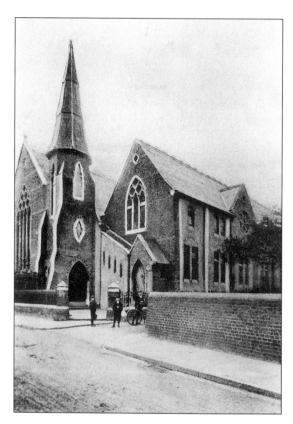

The Congregational Church in Crown Road at the corner of Beechwood Avenue was built in the late 1800s. For a number of years it stood unused until the Boy Scouts used it for their meetings. It was subsequently badly damaged by fire and was demolished in 1992.

Records show that the Bowling Club at Milton was founded before 1540 as a Crown Green. In 1925 the ground next to it was cleared and new turf laid which was donated by Edward Lloyd Ltd. It then became a three rink green and in 1939 it became as associated green – it is the second oldest in the country.

Meads Mill in Vicarage Road belonged to a Mr Watson. There was also a house known as Watson's Cottage which had a garden and about two acres of apple orchard. It is now part of Milton recreation ground and Martin Clarke's gymnasium.

"THE MEADS".

How the Meads looked in 1905 including, on the left, the grand old windmill. The path on the other side of the water is Vicarage Road which comes to the hill that now leads into Bobbing Village.

In the days when the windmill stood proudly pointing its sails towards the sky. The three pretty little girls sitting on the grass in front of it were perhaps the Miller's daughters.

50

The Meads Windmill was built around 1800 but became redundant at the start of the First World War. Around 1965 it was struck by lightning and what was left of it was later demolished.

Milton Church was built around 1070 and has one of the largest church towers in Kent. The pond in front of the church was known as Cornfords Pond and in the early 1900s people used it as a skating rink.

Built in Vicarage Road was this nice old house standing in its own grounds. It became the Milton vicarage in the early 1800s and was demolished in 1970 to be replaced by the modern vicarage.

Vicarage Road in 1930 shows that start of the Vicarage Estate. Past the house, behind the fence and trees, is where the vicarage used to stand.

Four
The Creek

The Creek. The Port of Milton in 1907 when it was a very busy waterway and had its own Harbour Master. Maybe the men with the horse and cart have just come back from a fishing trip and are unloading their catch of the day.

In the background of this postcard you can see two structures of scaffolding and if you look at the picture below you will see what they are for.

They were for the building of the two cranes seen here in Lloyds Wharf.

Moored along the quayside of the Creek, some barges wait to be loaded or unloaded.

Over on the far side of the Creek there are some bales of paper that may have been unloaded from the barges.

This picture of the Creek was taken from the Milton side but in the background you can see the Smeed Dean Cement and Brick Works in Murston.

On the barge in the front of this picture you can see the thick ropes that were used and also their winch.

On the right hand side of the picture a truck or engine travels along the railway tracks by the side of a barge.

On the right at Lloyds Wharf the No. 1 crane is unloading bales of paper from a lighter.

This barge could either be going into the boat yard for repairs or is being launched as there are quite a few people watching.

The Creek, Sittingbourne.

Dating from 1910 this is a lovely restful picture with the barge smoothly sailing out along the Creek carrying its cargo.

Five

Military of the First World War

The 7th Middlesex Regiment marching down Hollybank Hill and along West Street during the First World War. The buildings on the left which included the Volunteers public house have all been demolished to make way for flats called "The Cloisters".

These soldiers belong to the 3rd Battalion Middlesex Regiment.

The machine gun section of the 9th Middlesex Regiment with the gun safely in place on the gun carriage in 1914.

The officers of the Royal Army Corps in Gore Court Park.

The Royal Army Medical Corps when they were camped at Gore Court Park in 1916. The big house was demolished in the 1920s.

Whitehall in Bell Road was used as the Voluntary Aid Detachment Hospital during the First World War.

The lady driving the lovely old motor car is Mrs Honeyball who was the Commandant at the hospital.

Some casualties of the First World War at the Voluntary Aid Detachment Hospital.

Some more wounded soldiers at Whitehall outside a big marquee that was used as part of the hospital.

Standing at ease with their rifles at their sides are the 8th Middlesex Recruits Musketry Party.

DON'T WORRY!
I'm Quite Comfortable at SITTINGBOURNE.

A soldier who was stationed in Sittingbourne during the First World War sent this postcard home to his mother in 1918 to let her know that he was alive and well.

Marching out of Berry Street into the High Street in 1914 is D Company of the 9th Middlesex Regiment with their rifles on their left shoulders.

These soldiers marching down the street have their rifles strapped onto their backs. On the left by the lamp post is the opening of Crescent Street and the shop with the big advertising board is now the electricity showroom.

A military funeral going along West Street during the First World War. The deceased must have been a soldier of high rank or someone who was very well known in the town. On the right stands the Railway Tavern public house which is now known as the Ypres Tavern.

Unveiling of the war memorial in 1921 at the recreation ground in memory of the men who sacrificed their lives in the First World War. As you can see, a lot of people turned up for this momentous occasion.

Six

Murston Tong and Bapchild

Murston Creek dated 1914 shows the old cement works and beyond them the old gas works. On the left is the Brickmakers Arms public house which is the only building left standing although now derelict.

Sadly this is all that is left of the old church which stands at the end of the Church Road in Murston. It is a very ancient church that was built around the thirteenth century and is now in poor repair.

All Saints' church in Murston is known as the new church although it was opened in 1874. The roof which is on the top of the tower in this picture is no longer there.

Murston war memorial was erected in memory of the men of Murston who lost their lives in the First World War. It stands near the church in front of the Village Hall.

Murston Rectory, which was built in 1867 and once stood in 17 acres of park land, was a gift of St John's College Cambridge. Now standing on the site is the Canterbury Road Housing Estate.

The post office and village shop in Church Road, Murston. The house next to the post box used to be Murston's first schoolroom. Demolished in 1964, the site is now the entrance to the Sittingbourne Football Ground which was built in 1993.

Ebenezer Villas stood on the west side of Church Road in Murston and was the home of Mr Norris Andrews and Mr John William Andrews around the turn of the century. The house was demolished many years ago.

St Giles church at Tong is built in early-Norman and early-English style with a thirteenth-century tower which holds three bells. The path that runs along the side of the church is now surrounded by tall trees and bushes and the house that stood on the opposite side of the road to the church is no longer there.

This picture is dated 1909 and shows Tong church which is dedicated to St Giles. This part of Tong has changed little over the years.

New Road in Tong leads from Tong mill to St Giles church. Under the railway bridge on the left is the road that leads into Tong Road, Murston.

Sittingbourne   *Winter scene at Tong*

Here is a beautiful winter scene at Tong. The building standing on the right used to be a bakery belonging to the Wicks family. It has two different dates on it – one 1837 and the other 1866.

The spring that feeds Tong Pond is called the Becketts Spring because it was a very popular stopping place for the Pilgrims on their way to Canterbury Cathedral.

Tong Pond in the 1950s when it was used as a boating lake – what a nice way to spend a sunny afternoon!

Bapchild Street after a snowfall in 1906. All the people are standing there to have their photograph taken – even the dog sitting in the horse cart is posing for the camera! Standing on the left is the Fox and Goose public house which was built in 1887.

Radfield House is situated on the main road between Sittingbourne and Teynham. Many years ago it used to have a Free Chapel.

Bapchild Church is dedicated to St Laurence and has a lovely thirteenth-century tower and pointed spire.

Bapchild Village facing west towards Sittingbourne. It looks as if some of the lads are going for a bicycle ride.

Bapchild Vicarage & Church, Nr. Sittingbourne.   Photo. F. L. Robinson, Sittingbo

The old vicarage in School Lane, Bapchild in 1908. It stands on the opposite side of the road to the church that can be seen in the background.

Two little boys are busy playing in the lane at Bapchild in 1902. The building behind them is the Bapchild and Tong school.

These children walking along the lane in Bapchild are dressed in their Sunday best and look as if they have been to Sunday school at St Laurence church which is on the right at the bottom of the lane.

Seven
Leisure and Schools

With the band playing, hundreds of people are strolling along the High Street on their way to the Albany Road Meadows. They are going to one of the Co-operative Society's demonstration and children's fêtes that were held each year – this one was on 13 July 1920.

Sittingbourne division of the Salvation Army in 1932. The name, "Sittingbourne" is printed across their flag.

Here is the Salvation Army again. This time they are wearing different uniforms, the year is 1943 and Sittingbourne is printed across their drum.

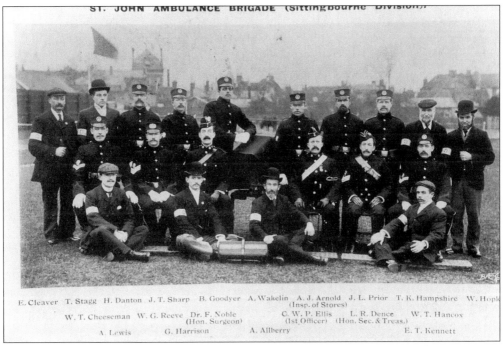

The Sittingbourne division of the St John Ambulance Brigade which was formed in 1904.

The St John Ambulance Brigade, Doddington division in 1905. The name "Doddington" is on the two medical bags.

A street party was held for some of the children who lived on the Vicarage Estate, Milton to celebrate the Coronation of Queen Elizabeth in 1953. A good time was had by all!

Feeding 400 children at one of the Co-op's annual demonstration fêtes. Judging by the lovely clothes they are wearing it must have been in the early 1900s.

The new Borden Grammar School in Remembrance Avenue just after it was built. The opening ceremony took place on Friday 11 October 1929 and was conducted by Lord Harris.

Smartly dressed in their school uniforms, these are some of the boys who were taught at the Borden Grammar School.

St Michael's Mission School in East Street closed in 1958 and the pupils were transferred to South Avenue. The Shell service station together with the forecourt and the Ford car showroom now stand on the site.

The Council School in East Street in 1905 which is still in use today. It can also be seen in the background of the picture above.

The Convent of the Nativity in West Street at the corner of Ufton Lane was opened in 1894 and was run by the nuns until 1988. It closed in September 1993.

Inside one of the classrooms. Look how big the desks and chairs are and notice the lack of room between them.

Here are some of the girls from the Convent School in the school grounds. It was also a boarding school for some of the pupils until the mid-1980s.

Another postcard of the girls in the school grounds with the school in the background.

Boys in the playground of Milton Regis Council School which was built in 1898. This postcard was given to a boy who used to attend this school for old time's sake.

Tunstall Primary School was built in 1846, was enlarged in 1894 to accommodate 65 children and is still in use today.

Murston School with the Lushington Cottages on the right which were demolished long ago. While houses have been built on their site, the school is still in use as an infants school.

A classroom of infants at Murston School which was built in 1868 with just two classrooms. By 1905 three more classrooms had been added and it was extended again in 1959.

The swimming baths were opened in July 1896 by Mr Frank Lloyd who contributed the largest amount of money for construction.

This is how the swimming baths in St Michael's Road had been transformed in 93 years. This picture was taken just before their demolition in 1989.

At Gore Court Football Ground in 1909, with a boys match in progress.

THE CRICKET FIELD, NR. SITTINGBOURNE. 5712

The cricket ground at the Grove in Key Street with the pavilion standing on the left.

The Sittingbourne Recreation Ground in Albany Road opened in 1882 but this picture is dated 1906.

This lovely old postcard dated 1907 shows the thatched summer house in the recreation Ground. Notice all the young ladies outside the summer house with their sun hats on.

Another picture of the old thatched summer house which was sadly pulled down in the early 1960s.

The recreation ground in 1928 with the war memorial standing on the right which was moved into Central Avenue in 1989.

Eight

Teynham and Lynsted

Standing in Teynham at the corner of Station Road was this nice old shop and garage that belonged to Mr W Rye. In the shop he sold bicycles and behind it was the garage where he repaired cars. These is a man driving a lovely old car along the road by the garage – we wonder if it could have been Mr Rye trying out a car he had just repaired.

Green Street, Teynham in 1903. On the right stands the Lynsted Memorial which reads, "A.D. In the worship of God and Loyalty to the Throne the memorial was set up with offerings from the Parishes of Teynham and Lynsted in the year of the Queen's Diamond Jubilee".

New Gardens at Teynham was a beautiful old house, full of character. It was built around the sixteenth century and belonged to Mr and Mrs Honeyball but was demolished to make way for a housing estate.

Cherry picking near Sittingbourne in 1902. It must have been hard work climbing those tall ladders wearing long skirts.

This picture was taken at Hales Farm in Teynham. The men are weighing the cherries and getting them ready to go to market in 1909.

Hop Picking near Sittingbourne.

This lovely old postcard from 1908 was taken in the hop gardens near Sittingbourne. In those days the whole family used to go hop picking.

Strawberry fields near Sittingbourne.

Strawberry pickers in the fields near Sittingbourne in 1905.

Lynsted Lane. The house on the left is called Holly Bank House and is dated 1880 while the house that stands behind the tree is No 9 Providence House.

Old House, Lynsted.

The Old House, Lynsted, also called Anchor House, stands in a prime position at the corner of Ludgate Lane.

Standing on the right of this quiet country lane at Lynsted is the Black Lion public house.

This picture of Lynsted is a typical Kentish village scene from the early 1900s. The horse is standing outside the forge, perhaps waiting to be shod.

Nine
Borden Tunstall and Bredgar

Looking out across the horizon from the tower of Borden church in the days when there was more open countryside with leafy lanes and country cottages. The Maypole Inn is on the left with its nice neat hedge running along the garden and just beyond that is the playing field.

Borden church is dedicated to St Peter and St Paul and has a Norman tower and doorway. Inside the church there is a monument to Robert Plot, a historian who died in 1696.

Standing on the left of this picture of Borden Village is the Maypole Inn which dates from the early nineteenth century. The big house on the right was built in 1823 for the trustees of the Barrow Trust.

Borden Hall stands just behind the church. In the 1700s the Napleton family, major landowners, lived there.

A view inside Borden Hall in 1908 reveals its lovely old oak beams on the ceiling and some beautiful china in the dresser.

Robert Plot was born at Sutton Baron Farm in 1640 and grew up to become an antiquarian and natural historian. Roman remains were found at Sutton Baron Farm in the 1800s by Mr George Payne.

In Oad Street, Borden, stands the Wesleyan chapel that was built in 1858 and closed in the 1980s.

Tunstall church is dedicated to St John the Baptist – parts of this church were built in the thirteenth century.

The Hales monument in the Hales chapel inside Tunstall church was formerly erected to cover the centre of the fifteenth-century window in the south wall of the chapel.

Tunstall is a very pretty, well-kept country village not looking dissimilar from this picture dated 1916.

This is Tunstall Lane often used for a leisurely stroll to Sittingbourne.

Bredgar Village in 1904, situated about three miles south west of Sittingbourne. On the right stands the village post office with a nice old lamp above the doorway and just beyond that is the church dedicated to St John Baptist and partially built in the Norman period.

How Bredgar looked in the 1930s with the village post office on the left.

Bredgar Village Pond is on the right and just beyond that on the other side of the road stands the war memorial.

A lovely old postcard dated 1905 of Bredgar church.

Bredgar church and village in the 1920s. Down the lane is a horse and cart with a group of children standing round it, possibly hoping for a ride.

These old cottages opposite the church were the Holy Trinity College from the early fifteenth century. They later become known as the Chantry Houses and have now been demolished.

Silver Street in Bredgar in 1906 provides a lovely view of country life.

Ten
Industry, Shops and Transport

A close-up picture of the gas works in Milton which opened in 1932 and were built on the site of an old gas works dating from 1840. In the 1940s and 1950s people used to go to the gas works with wheelbarrows and old prams to buy coke which was a cheap fuel for their fires. All that is left now is part of the front office while the rest of the site is occupied by Milton Pipes.

Sittingbourne and Kemsley light railway used to belong to the paper mills and ran between the two mills and Ridham Dock. It now only runs to Kemsley Down as a tourist attraction.

Kemsley Mill in the early 1930s before the concrete water tower was built and when there were only four paper-making machines.

Inside Kemsley Paper Mill in 1927 showing No 1 and No 2 paper-making machines.

Kemsley log piles show the scale of the operation.

The logs were unloaded from the boats at Ridham Dock in buckets that tipped up to create the piles – this method is no longer used.

Some of the reels of paper that have been loaded on to one of the barges in 1932.

Damage caused by the heavy floods at Ridham Dock in 1953 – the Docks have since been partially rebuilt.

The big clean-up operation at the Kemsley Mill after the floods is about to start.

One of the many boats that sail into Ridham Dock.

Kemsley Mill on 12 August 1967 shows the men busy unloading the lorry and putting the logs neatly on the railway truck.

Sittingbourne Mill when it was called the Daily Chronicle Paper Mill (at the turn of the century).

The great fire at Sittingbourne Mill in 1907. Although the mill was badly damaged, none of the workers were laid off as they were given jobs repairing the fire damage.

Round the other side of the paper mill, Jubilee Street, was a popular street for children to play in.

One of the paper-making machines inside Sittingbourne Mill as the men have their picture taken.

In the early 1900s men are busy working on the No 9 and No 10 paper-making machines.

This is the reeler room where the reels of paper are cut to size ready to go to the printing presses.

Whitehall Preserve Works and Jam Factory was in Bell Road and was owned by Mr George Dean. It later become Peters Pie Factory then Freshbakes Pie Factory but has since made way for a housing estate.

Bugges Insecticide Factory which was demolished in 1994. It stood in the London Road opposite the Rhode House service station.

Brickfield, Murston Nr. Sittingbourne.

Smeed Deans brick fields at Murston and the sheds where the bricks were dried. It has all disappeared now the Eurolink Industrial Estate stands on the site.

Highstead chalk quarry in 1915. The chalk dug out from this quarry was washed then pumped through underground pipes to the cement and brick works at Murston.

The ladies and girls who used to work at the Queens Laundry when it was up the alleyway opposite St Michael's Church. Back row (left to right): Vinne Cooper, Joan Risbridger, Connie Feaver, Edna Goodman and Mrs Sterling. Middle row: Joyce Jarrot, Peggy Slingsby and Joan Fisher. Front row: Joan Hardy.

Mr Fred Mockett in his shop at 33 Frederick Street. He was also a greengrocer and fruiterer and was in business from 1933 to 1983. Mockett Court, at the top of Frederick Street, was named after Mr and Mrs Mockett.

Mr Henry Tett's ironmongers shop stood at No 61 High Street. He had a good window display and a number of oil lamps hang above the doorway.

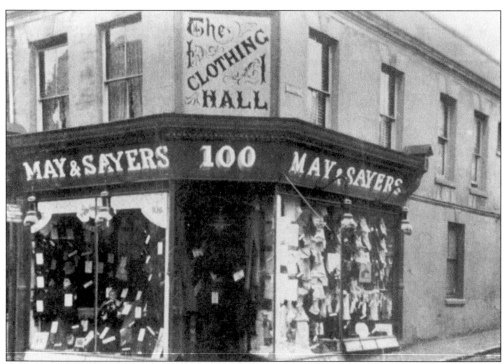

May and Sayers Clothing Hall at No 100 High Street was at the corner of Berry Street before it moved to No 78. It was an outfitters shop and specialised in school outfits.

The Dress House at No 30 High Street had previously been Marsh Ltd. It was a draper and milliner shop as well as a ladies outfitters and furnishers.

The hops have been dried in the oast house and are now ready to go to the brewery.

Hops loaded on to the lorry outside the oast houses in Bell Road in 1932. Standing by the lorry door is Mr Gammon and the little girls are Joyce Sills and Joyce Gammon while on the engine is Fred Heathfield and one of the men on the cab is Cliff Harris.

Sittingbourne railway station in 1909. The railway-line from London reached here in 1958 and continued on to Faversham in 1860.

Thankfully it does not take a day to reach Sheerness by train!

An old dustcart from the days when Milton had its own Rural District Council. There were no wheelie bins in those days – only the old metal dustbins which were collected from the back yards, emptied and then returned to where they were taken from.

This 1919 van belonged to Mr Blundy who used to have a sweet shop in Milton High Street. It was next to the alley that led to the recreation ground so on their way to play on the swings the children would eat their sweets or lollies.

One of the two old Sentinel steam wagons that belonged to Lloyds Paper Mill in Sittingbourne in the 1930s.

A familiar sight on the roads between Sittingbourne and Kemsley in the 1960s and 1970s were the big red Bowaters lorries which were used to transport paper to the printing presses in London.

This Sentinel steam wagon used to belong to Wills and Packham who were brick manufacturers.

A furniture van belonging to John Peters and Sons who had a furniture shop at Nos 17-19 High Street next to the East Kent Gazette Office.

A lovely old horse-drawn bakery cart that belonged to the Co-operative Society. It must have been around the turn of the century and the delivery man looks smart in his pin stripe suit and tie.

A 1920s motorbike and sidecar that we believe belonged to the photographer who was so proud of it he made sure it was in most of the pictures he took.